# Collins

# Easy Learning

# First phonics

My name is ...................................................................... .

I am .................. years old.

## Carol Medcalf

# How to use this book

- Find a quiet, comfortable place to work, away from other distractions.

- This book has been written in a logical order, so start at the first page and work your way through.

- Help with reading the instructions where necessary, and ensure that your child understands what to do.

- This book is a gentle introduction to 29 of the 44 sounds of the English language. Working through the book, your child will start to realise that words are made up of small separate sounds. These individual sounds are called phonemes; bus, for example, is made up of three phonemes: b-u-s. Encourage your child to sound out each letter sound before they attempt to read the whole word. For example, say 'kuh-a-tuh' and then read 'cat'. Some sounds are represented by two letters (digraph), such as sh. For these sounds your child should sound out the single sh sound and not the individual letter sounds.

- If an activity is too difficult for your child then do more of our suggested practical activities (see Activity note) and return to the page when you know that they're likely to achieve it.

- Always end each activity before your child gets tired so that they will be eager to return next time.

- Help and encourage your child to check their own answers as they complete each activity.

- Let your child return to their favourite pages once they have been completed. Talk about the activities they enjoyed and what they have learnt.

## Special features of this book:

- **Activity note:** situated at the bottom of every left-hand page, this suggests further activities and encourages discussion about what your child has learnt.

- **Phonics panel:** situated at the bottom of every right-hand page, this builds up the phonetic alphabet by showing pictures that start with each letter sound from a to z, plus pictures for the sh, ch and ck sounds. Use this to recap the 29 sounds taught in this book.

- **Certificate:** the certificate on page 24 should be used to reward your child for their effort and achievement. Remember to give them plenty of praise and encouragement, regardless of how they do.

Published by Collins
An imprint of HarperCollinsPublishers
77–85 Fulham Palace Road
Hammersmith
London
W6 8JB

Browse the complete Collins catalogue at
www.collins.co.uk

First published in 2006
© HarperCollinsPublishers 2008

11

ISBN 978-0-00-730086-0

The author asserts the moral right to be identified as the author of this work.

British Library Cataloguing in Publication Data

A Catalogue record for this publication is available from the British Library.

Written by Carol Medcalf
Design and layout by Lodestone Publishing Limited, Uckfield, East Sussex; www.lodestonepublishing.com
Illustrated by Jenny Tulip
Cover design by Susi Martin
Cover illustration by John Haslam
Printed and bound in China

# Contents

# Letter sounds

Draw lines to match the letter sounds to the pictures.

k

h

j

l

i

m

# More letter sounds

● Draw lines to match the letter sounds to the pictures.

A good starting point for learning and understanding phonetic sounds is to talk about your child's name (if it starts with a phonetic sound!). Also discuss their friends' names and try to find a name for each letter sound from a to z, for example: Abbie, Ben, Carl, Dev, Edward, etc.

x

t

v

z

y

w

u

# Start sounds a to d

- Say the word for each picture. Draw a (circle) round the letter sound it starts with.

a   (b)   c   d

a   b   c   d

a   b   c   d

a   b   c   d

- Say the word for each picture. Write the letter sound it starts with.

a

# Start sounds e to h

- Say the word for each picture. Draw a circle round the letter sound it starts with.

| | | | |
|---|---|---|---|
| e | f | g | h |
| e | f | g | h |
| e | f | g | h |
| e | f | g | h |

- Say the word for each picture. Write the letter sound it starts with.

# Practice time!

- Look at the letter in each set. Draw a circle round the pictures that start with the letter sound.

Further develop your child's listening skills by making musical instruments and playing with them together. Put an instrument behind your back – can your child guess which one it is based on the sound it makes?

# Start sounds i to l

Say the word for each picture. Draw a circle round the letter sound it starts with.

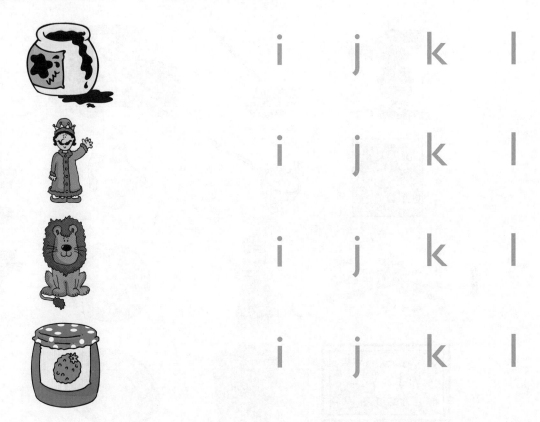

i     j     k     l

i     j     k     l

i     j     k     l

i     j     k     l

Draw lines to match the pictures to the correct start sound.

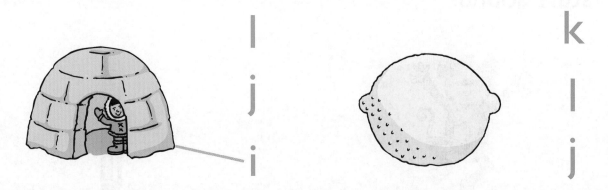

l

j

i

k

l

j

# Start sounds m to p

- Look at the letter in each row. Cross out the picture that does not start with the letter sound.

m

n

o

p

- Draw lines to match the pictures to the correct start sound.

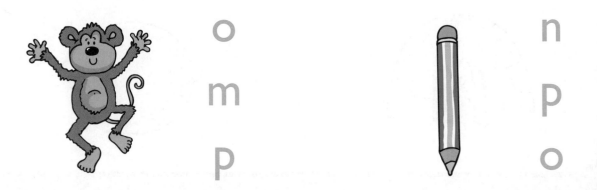

o

m

p

n

p

o

x

Emphasize the first sound in words. Say: 'tttttt-rain, sssss-nake, rrrrr-ed'.

# Practice time!

- Look at the letter in each set. Draw a (circle) round the pictures that start with the letter sound.

# Start sounds q to s

- Draw lines to match the pictures to the correct start sound.

- Say the word for each picture. Write the letter sound it starts with.

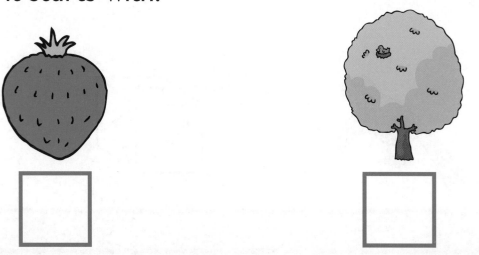

# Start sounds t to w

Look at the letter in each set. Draw a (circle) round the pictures that start with the letter sound.

t

v

w

u

# Start sounds x to z

● Say the word for each picture. Draw a circle round the letter sound it starts with.

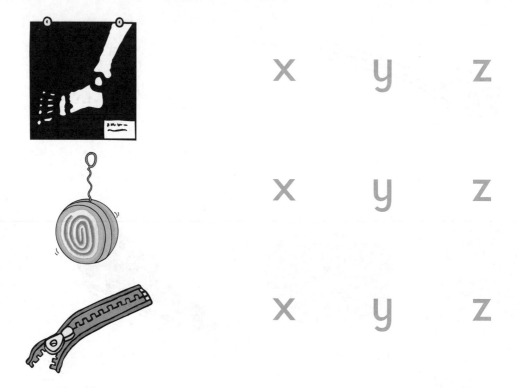

x     y     z

x     y     z

x     y     z

● Say the word for each picture. Write the letter sound it starts with.

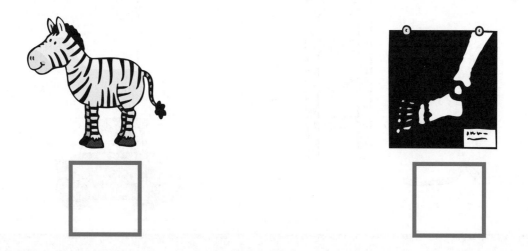

When reading a familiar story with a repetitive word in it, for example Cinderella, say: 'every time you hear the word Cinderella shout bananas'. This helps to develop your child's concentration and listening skills.

# Same letter sounds

Say the word for each picture. Draw lines to match the pictures that start with the same start sounds.

# End letter sounds

Say the word for each picture. Choose the correct letter sound to finish the word. Write the letter.

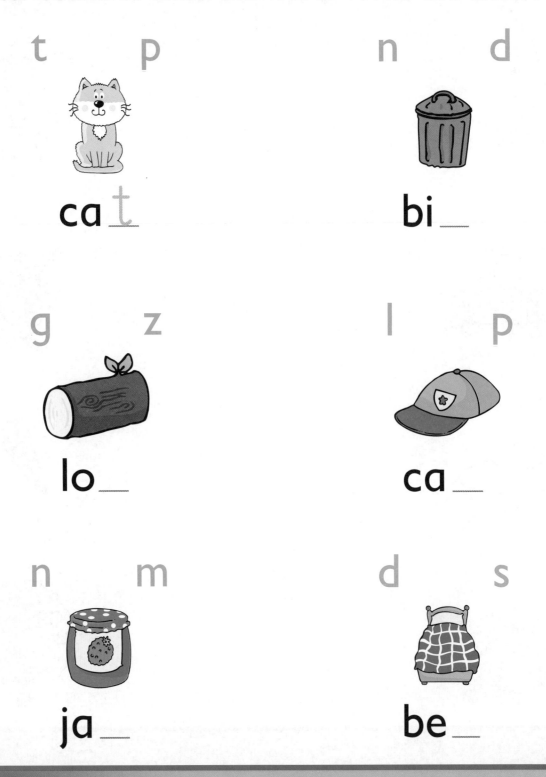

t      p

**ca** t

n      d

**bi** __

g      z

**lo** __

l      p

**ca** __

n      m

**ja** __

d      s

**be** __

When doing this activity ask your child: 'What sound can you hear at the end of the word cat?' Use the phonetic alphabet and say: c.a.t, emphasizing the last sound. Say the words with both endings shown. Ask: 'Is it c.a.t or c.a.p?'

# Same end letter sounds

Say the words for the pictures in each row. Draw a (circle) round the letter that makes the end sound of these words.

p    d

g    m

c    m

t    x

# sh

Look at the pictures and say the words. Write the missing sh letters.

sh ip        _ _op        _ _oe

Colour the pictures that have the sh sound in the word.

Play voice games together. Say: 'Can you make your voice go down a slide? Wheeeeee. Hiss like a snake, hissss. Talk quietly and say shhhhh. Sound surprised and say oooooooo.' This will help your child to pronounce letter sounds.

Look at the pictures and say the words. Write the missing ch letters.

lun____

wit____

____icken

Colour the pictures that have the ch sound in the word.

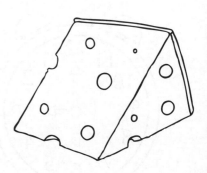

# ck

- Look at the pictures and say the words. Write the missing ck letters.

du_ _          so_ _          bla_ _

- Colour the pictures that have the ck sound in the word.

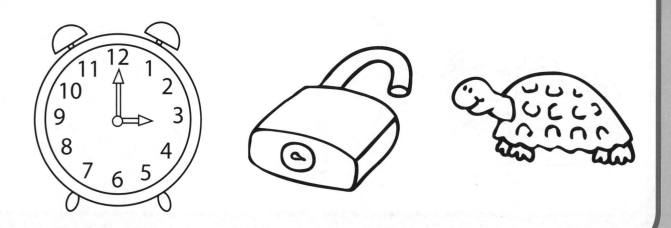

Make a sound collection by gathering toys/objects that start with the same phonemes (letter sound), for example 'b': a toy bus, ball, bat, book, balloon and boat. See how many different collections of phonetic sound piles you can make.

# Which sound?

- Say the word for each picture. Choose the correct sounds to finish the word. Write the letters.

sh        ch

fi___

sh        ck

du___

ck        ch

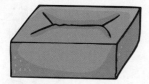

bri___

ch        sh

___op

sh        ck

clo___

ck        ch

wit___

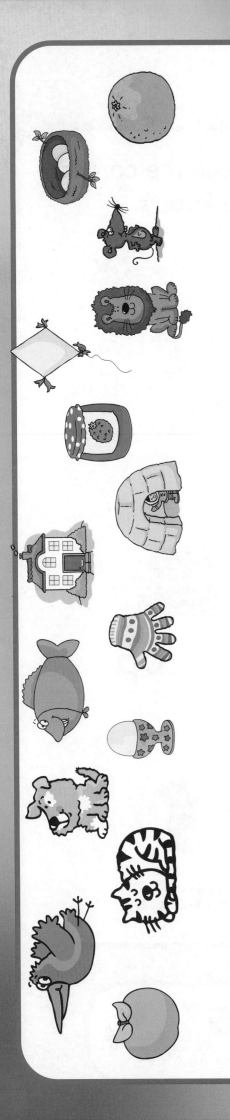

Well done ............... (name)

You have finished!

Now you know your letter sounds!

Date ...............

Age ...............

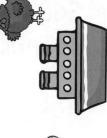